A Kid's Guide to Origami™

Making ORIGAMI PUZZLES Step by Step

Michael G. LaFosse

The Rosen Publishing Group's
PowerKids Press™
New York

To Jeannine Mosely

Published in 2004 by The Rosen Publishing Group, Inc.
29 East 21st Street, New York, NY 10010

First Edition

Editor: Jannell Khu
Book Design: Emily Muschinske
Layout Design: Kim Sonsky

Illustration Credits: Michael G. LaFosse
Photo Credits: All photographs by Adriana Skura.

LaFosse, Michael G.
Making origami puzzles step by step / Michael G. LaFosse.
    v. cm. — (A kid's guide to origami)
Includes bibliographical references and index.
Contents: What is origami? — Lighting bolt octahedron — Alexander's tulip puzzle box — Cube corner puzzle — Celebration puzzle box — Fortune cookie puzzle box — Sailboat wreath puzzle box — Tile frame puzzle — Finger pinwheel puzzle.
ISBN 0-8239-6704-2 (library binding)
1. Origami—Juvenile literature. 2. Puzzles—Juvenile literature. [1. Origami. 2. Puzzles. 3. Paper work. 4. Handicraft.] I. Title. II. Series.
TT870 .L2342267 2004
736'.982—dc21

                                           2002153461

Manufactured in the United States of America

Contents

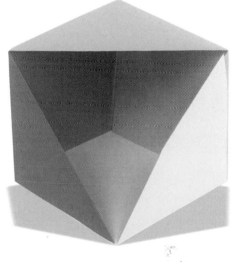

What Is Origami?

Origami is the art of folding paper to make shapes. It is an art and a craft enjoyed by people of all ages throughout the world. You can **categorize** origami into many specialties such as paper airplanes, toys, animals, masks, boxes, games, and puzzles. Most origami projects are folded from a single piece of paper. However, to make the origami puzzles in this book, you will use more than one piece of paper.

Origami puzzles are also called **modular** origami. This means that origami puzzles are made with separate origami parts that you put together to make one puzzle. Modular origami is quickly becoming one of the most popular specialties of paper origami.

Some of the puzzles will be **challenging** to make and put together. However, learning the origami key before you start will make it easier for you to fold the puzzles. The origami key is at the back of this book on page 22. Use the origami key as well as the directions under each drawing.

Make these puzzles with different kinds of paper. If you are using origami paper, start with the white side facing up. Many kinds of printer and gift-wrap papers are also good for making origami puzzles. Enjoy the challenge of making these puzzles. Some day, perhaps you will design your own puzzles!

Eight-Sided Puzzle

An octahedron is a shape that has eight sides. A word that begins with "oct" has something to do with the number eight. For example, the sea creature named the octopus has eight legs! October was the eighth month of the Roman calendar. Octahedron Puzzles make great **ornaments** for Christmas. Make several of these shapes, thread a string through one end of each shape, and hang them on your Christmas tree. Try different color combinations for this puzzle. Write a message on the completed puzzle, take it apart, and send it to a friend. Your friend will have fun putting the octahedron puzzle together to read your message.

1

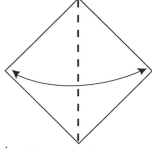

Use four 8-inch- (20.3-cm-) square papers. Position the paper so that it is diamond shaped. Valley fold the paper from left to right to make a center crease line. The dotted lines are guides to show you where you should fold the paper. Unfold it.

2

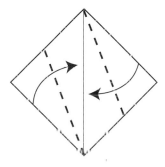

Valley fold the bottom left edge and the top right edge to the crease line.

3

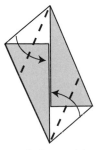

Valley fold the the top left and bottom right edges to the crease line.

4

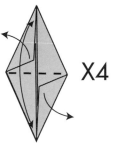

X4

Valley fold the paper in half, bottom corner to top corner, and unfold. Unfold halfway the two short edges of paper, to lift them straight up. Repeat these steps for the other three squares of paper. You will need four to make one puzzle.

5

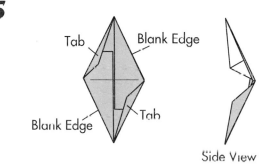

Tab   Blank Edge

Blank Edge   Tab

Side View

Each piece has two tabs and two blank edges. Each piece should be bent a little, in the middle (see side view).

6

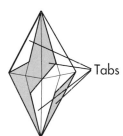

Tabs

Build this puzzle by placing all eight tabs over all eight blank edges. All of the tabs must be on the outside.

Tulip Puzzle Box

This puzzle is made with two pieces of paper. The two puzzle pieces look like the tops of tulip flowers. The tulip shapes fit together to make an origami puzzle box. This Tulip Puzzle Box can be put together in several ways to make different color patterns. The patterns are **determined** by how many corners of the top box get tucked inside the bottom box. Try experimenting with different colored papers. Place a surprise gift inside the Tulip Puzzle Box such as chocolates, dried flowers, or small toys.

1

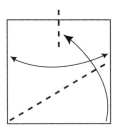

Use two 8-inch- (20.3-cm-) square papers. Fold one paper's top in half, edge to edge, to make a pinch mark at its middle. Unfold it. Fold the lower right corner to meet the pinch mark.

2

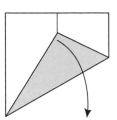

Your paper should look like this. Unfold it. The crease line you made is important.

3

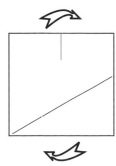

Now your paper should look like this. Rotate the paper one quarter turn to the right. After rotating it, the last crease line you made should be positioned as shown below in step 4.

4

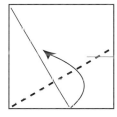

Valley fold the bottom end of the square. Notice that the fold is angled. Use the dotted lines and the right pinch mark as guides to make this fold. Also look ahead at step 5 to see how the shape should appear.

5

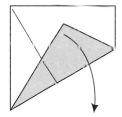

Your paper should look like this. Unfold the paper.

6

Repeat steps 3 through 5 on the last two edges of the square. Turn the paper over.

7

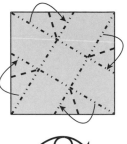

Notice the four areas where there are valley fold lines. One area at a time, carefully push the dotted lines inward and mountain fold the paper to make a neat crease. Do this for each valley fold area. When you are done, you will have four box corners. Next turn the shape over.

8

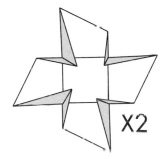

The tulip shape will look like the above. Repeat steps 1 through 7 with the other paper.

9

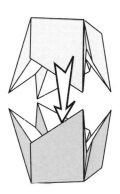

Fit the four corners of one box inside the four corners of the other box to complete the puzzle. This step is very tricky so take your time. The tricky part is what makes this box a puzzle!

Open Box Puzzle

Notice the opening of this origami puzzle. This opening allows you to push out the bottom flap and the two back corner flaps. The movable flaps allow something to pass from the inside to the outside. However, you can't push something from the outside to the inside, because the opening is one way. Take a real flower and insert the stem through the opening. Push the Open Box Puzzle down to the bottom of the stem, and place it on the table top. The Open Box Puzzle will act as a base to hold the flower upright. These Open Box Puzzles can be stacked to make a tower. How many can you stack before the tower falls? Can you discover other ways to join this puzzle? What can you build if you make several different-sized Open Box Puzzles? Have fun finding out!

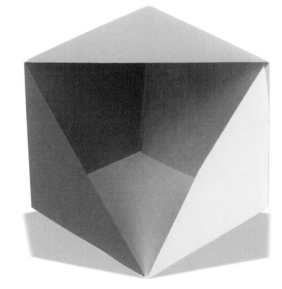

1

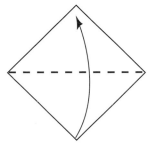

Use three 8-inch- (20.3-cm-) square papers (20.3 cm). Place the paper so that it looks like a diamond shape. Valley fold it in half, corner to corner, to make a triangle shape.

2

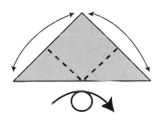

Fold up the left and the right corners to meet at the top corner. Unfold them and turn the paper over.

3

Mountain fold down the top corner of the first layer to the inside of the paper. Look ahead to step 4 to see the shape.

4

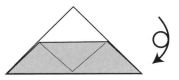

Turn the paper over. Next flip the paper so that the wide part is on top. Look at the step below for the shape.

5

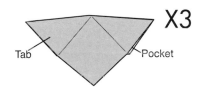

Repeat steps 1 through 5 with the other two pieces of paper. You are now ready to use the top left corner as a tab. The top right corner will be the pocket.

6

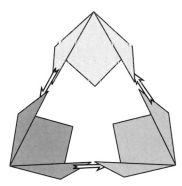

Insert the tab end of each puzzle piece into the pocket end of another. The back end will close in the shape of a cube corner. Experiment with more than three pieces of paper and see if you can invent other puzzle formations!

Celebration Puzzle Box

This origami box is called the **Celebration Puzzle Box** because you can fill it with colorful **confetti** or tiny **treasures**. The tabs hold the box together. However, because the box doesn't close very tightly, you can pop it open with a gentle hit, when you throw it into the air. Your friends will be surprised when they see a colorful shower of confetti fall out of the Celebration Puzzle Box.

This puzzle is as much fun to take apart as it is to put together. You can make bigger boxes from bigger paper. This puzzle is perhaps the most challenging puzzle in this book to fold. Smaller-sized papers work best when you are first learning how to make this puzzle. Take your time studying the directions.

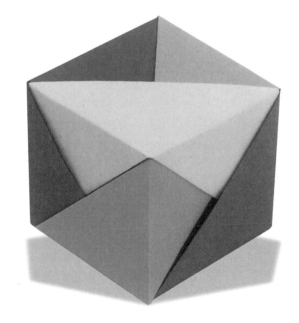

1

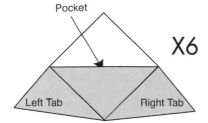

Make six puzzle units from the Open Box Puzzle on page 11. Notice that you will use both of the bottom corners as tabs for this origami Celebration Box. The pocket is the space behind the center folded triangle.

2

With one hand, hold the first puzzle piece in the position of the left piece shown in the drawing. Add a second piece by sliding the left tab into the top half of the pocket of the first piece.

3

Add the third piece by sliding the left tab under the left tab of the second piece. The right tab of the third piece should be behind the right tab of the first piece.

4

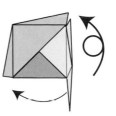

Position the right tab of the second piece to cover the square face of the third piece. Turn the box so that the bottom side faces you.

5

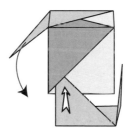

Add the fourth piece by sliding the right corner into the left half of the pocket, covering the right tab of the second piece.

6

Complete the box by turning it and adding pieces to the empty sides. If you do this correctly, all six sides of the box will display the pattern shown above in this step. To surprise a friend, throw the cube into the air and hit it with an upward swing of your palm. The box will fall apart and you can put it back together again. Have races to see who can build a box the fastest!

Fortune Cookie Puzzle Box

This puzzle box looks like a Chinese fortune cookie. Use this puzzle box to hold little gifts. The Fortune Cookie Puzzle Box also makes a wonderful holiday ornament. These boxes are especially pretty when folded from colorful gift-wrap papers. They can even be folded from wallpaper! Extra folds in this box help to display the colors on the corners. You can make tiny boxes and use them as beads. Each box has a small hole, through which you can pass a thread. After you string the boxes, you can wear them around your neck like a necklace. Once you learn how to fold this box, you will want to make many of them, because they are quick and easy.

1

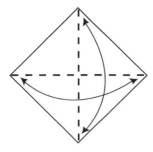

Use three 10-inch- (25.4-cm-) square papers. Position the paper so that it is diamond shaped. Valley fold it in half, in both directions, and unfold it.

2

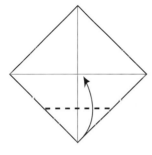

Valley fold up the bottom corner point to touch the center of the paper.

3

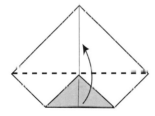

Fold up the bottom edge to the center of the paper. Use the dotted line as a guide.

4

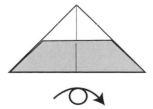

Your paper will look like this. Turn the paper over.

5

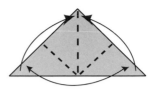

Fold the paper in half, right corner to left corner. Unfold it. Next fold up the left and the right corners to the top corner. Look at step 6 to see how the paper should appear.

6

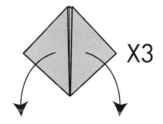

X3

Unfold the left and right corners that you made in the last step. Repeat these steps for the rest of the papers.

7

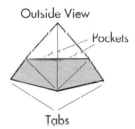

Outside View

Pockets

Tabs

The outside of each puzzle piece has mountain creases and two pockets. The half-square corners are the tabs.

8

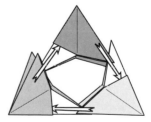

Slip both tabs of one puzzle piece into the pocket of another. Add the third piece the same way. All the valley creases face inside the box.

Wreath Puzzle Box

One unit of this **wreath resembles** the logo of the Origami Center of America in New York City. The center was founded by Lillian Oppenheimer in 1958. I designed this wreath in 1998, in honor of Oppenheimer's memory, to celebrate the fortieth **anniversary** of her origami center and what would have been her one hundredth birthday! Oppenheimer was one of the **pioneers** of origami in the United States. She **encouraged** origami artists to share their ideas and to write books about the art. Oppenheimer's work continues through the efforts of OrigamiUSA, New York.

1

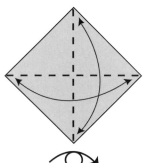

Use eight 10-inch (25.4-cm) squares of paper. Position the paper so that it is diamond shaped. Fold it in half, corner to corner. Unfold it. Repeat the folds in the other direction. Unfold the paper. Turn it over.

2

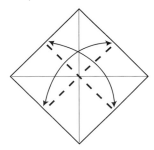

Fold in half, edge to edge, and unfold each way.

3

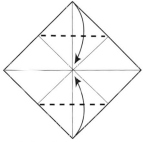

Fold the top and the bottom corners to meet at the center. Use the dotted lines as guides.

4

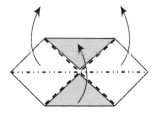

Use the mountain folds and valley folds made in steps 1 and 2 to form a sailboat shape. You will see that each white corner mountain folds in half to become a sail. Fold each sail separately, one coming up on the right and the other coming up on the left. The bottom edge of the paper will come up to meet the top edge.

5

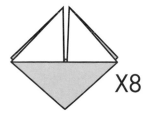

X8

This is the finished puzzle piece. Repeat these steps with the rest of the papers.

6

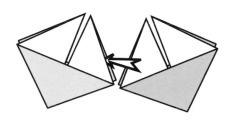

Join two puzzle pieces by slipping the left sail of one boat into the right sail of another.

7

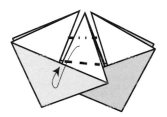

When the two sails are joined, valley fold and mountain fold the two down to make a tab.

8

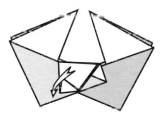

Tuck the tab into the boat that it covers. Now the boats are locked together.

9

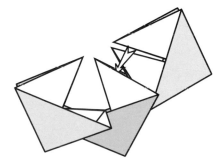

Add the rest of the puzzle pieces in the same way to make the wreath.

Frame Puzzle

The Frame Puzzle is a two-sided origami frame that has patterns on both sides. This origami shape is needed to fold the paddle element for the Finger Pinwheel Puzzle that you will learn how to fold in the next chapter. This is a great frame to make for paper **quilts**, signs, or banners. You can **laminate** the frames to make them **waterproof**. They make great drink coasters. Experiment with colors, and add other origami shapes that can be easily slipped inside several of the folds or pockets. The Frame Puzzle also makes a great **scrambled** message puzzle. Write a message all over the completed frame. Take the frame apart and give the pieces to a friend. Your friend will have fun trying to put the puzzle together to read your message.

1

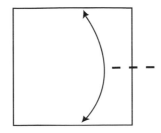

Use four squares of paper that measure 10 inches (25.4 cm) by 10 inches. Fold the right side in half to make a small pinch mark on the right side of the square.

2

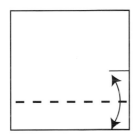

Fold up the bottom edge to the pinch mark. The pinch mark is in the middle of the square. Unfold the paper.

3

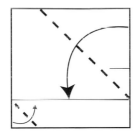

Fold up the lower left corner to the crease line. Fold down the upper right corner to the crease line.

4

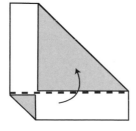

Use the crease to fold up the bottom edge.

5

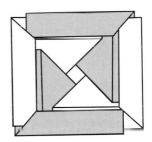

Repeat steps 1 through 5 with the other three pieces of paper. You will need four puzzle pieces to make one tile frame.

6

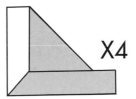

Form the tile frame by weaving the four puzzle pieces together. Look carefully at the drawing to see how to layer the papers. Notice that the square corners of the frame get tucked under the folded edges of the connecting puzzle pieces.

7

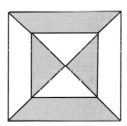

This is the completed puzzle's frame side.

8

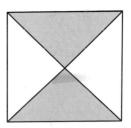

This is the completed puzzle's tile side.

Finger Pinwheel Puzzle

To make the Finger Pinwheel Puzzle, use only two colors of paper. You will need four pieces of each color of paper. You need to **alternate** the colors as you fold this project. The finished model will look almost like two frames weaving through each other. Make tiny pinwheels out of smaller papers and larger ones out of the biggest papers you can find!

1

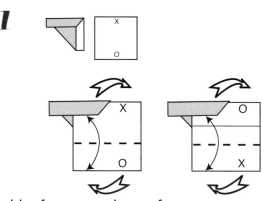

Fold a frame puzzle unit from page 18. Use eight 10-inch- (25.4-cm-) square papers. Slip one paper's edge under the frame's folded edge. Fold the paper's bottom edge up to meet the frame's edge. Unfold the paper, and repeat with its opposite edge. Remove the frame.

2

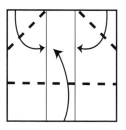

You will have two vertical valley creases. The distance between these creases is one-fourth of the length of the square. Position the paper so that the creases run from top to bottom. Fold down the top corners to the crease lines. Fold up the bottom edge to match the bottom edges of the triangles. Look ahead at step 3 for the shape.

3

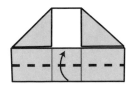

Valley fold up the bottom edge, carefully matching the top edge of the rectangle.

4

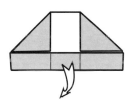

Unfold the bottom edge.

5

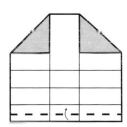

Valley fold up the bottom edge to the first crease line.

6

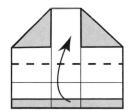

Use the top crease to fold up the bottom edge.

7

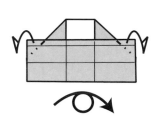

Mountain fold the corners over the sloping edges. Turn the paper over.

8

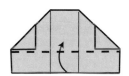

Valley fold up the bottom edge.

9

Mountain fold the vertical creases. These are the creases that you made in step 1.

10

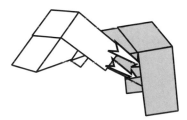

Fit the eight puzzle pieces together by slipping the square-shaped tabs under the two folded edges on each side of the unit.

Origami Key

1 MOUNTAIN FOLD

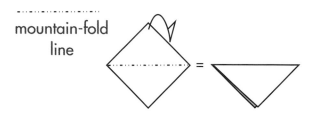

mountain-fold line

Notice the mountain fold line. To make a mountain fold, fold the paper back away from you, so that it meets at the other side.

2 VALLEY FOLD

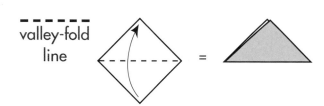

valley-fold line

Notice the valley fold line. To make a valley fold, fold the paper toward you.

3 MOVE, PULL, PUSH, SLIP

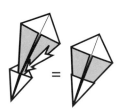

4 DIRECTION ARROW

5 FOLD and UNFOLD

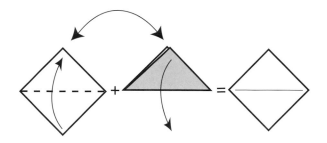

6 TURNOVER

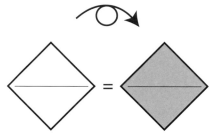

7 ROTATE

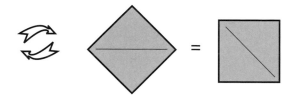

8 CUT

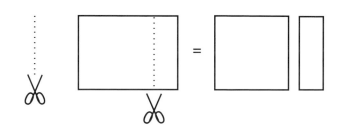

9 REPEAT

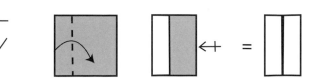

Glossary

alternate (OL-tur-nayt) To take turns.

anniversary (a-nuh-VERS-ree) The date on which an event occurred in the past or its special observance.

categorize (KA-tih-guh-ryz) To group or class things.

celebration (seh-luh-BRAY-shun) Observance of special times, with activities.

challenging (CHA-lenj-ing) Requiring extra effort.

confetti (kun-FEH-tee) Very small pieces of colored paper.

determined (dih-TER-mind) Being very focused on doing something.

encouraged (in-KUR-ijd) Gave hope, cheer, or certainty to.

laminate (LA-meh-nayt) To seal with plastic covering.

modular (MAH-jeh-ler) Made of many parts.

ornaments (OR-nuh-ments) Decorations.

pioneers (py-uh-NEERZ) People who start or help to open up new ideas or things in new places.

quilts (KWILTZ) Bed coverings made of two layers of cloth and stuffed with soft fabric. The cloths are held together by crisscrossed lines of sewing.

resembles (rih-ZEM-bulz) Looks like.

scrambled (SKRAM-buld) Mixed together.

treasures (TREH-zherz) Things of great worth or value.

waterproof (WAH-ter-proof) Not able to get wet.

wreath (REETH) A circle of leaves and sometimes flowers woven together.

Index

Web Sites

Due to the changing nature of Internet links, PowerKids Press has developed an online list of Web sites related to the subject of this book. This site is updated regularly. Please use this link to access the list:
www.powerkidslinks.com/kgo/puzzles/